11-95

# THE
# KIOWA
# INDIANS

THE JUNIOR LIBRARY OF
AMERICAN INDIANS

# THE
# KIOWA
# INDIANS

*Terrance Dolan*

CHELSEA HOUSE PUBLISHERS
*New York  Philadelphia*

FRONTISPIECE: *Kiowa Flute Dancer,* painted in watercolor by Kiowa artist Stephen Mopope in 1933.

CHAPTER TITLE ORNAMENT: A symbol painted on the shield belonging to members of the Owl Doctor Society. The men in this organization had the gift of prophecy.

**Chelsea House Publishers**
EDITORIAL DIRECTOR Richard Rennert
EXECUTIVE MANAGING EDITOR Karyn Gullen Browne
EXECUTIVE EDITOR Sean Dolan
COPY CHIEF Robin James
PICTURE EDITOR Adrian G. Allen
ART DIRECTOR Robert Mitchell
MANUFACTURING DIRECTOR Gerald Levine
PRODUCTION COORDINATOR Marie Claire Cebrián-Ume

**The Junior Library of American Indians**
SENIOR EDITOR Terrance Dolan

**Staff for THE KIOWA INDIANS**
COPY EDITOR Nicole Greenblatt
EDITORIAL ASSISTANT Joy Sanchez
ASSISTANT DESIGNER John Infantino
PICTURE RESEARCHER Sandy Jones
COVER ILLUSTRATOR Hal Just

3 5 7 9 8 6 4 2

**Library of Congress Cataloging-in-Publication Data**

Dolan, Terrance.
The Kiowa Indians / Terrance Dolan.
  p. cm.—(The Junior Library of American Indians)
Includes index.
      ISBN 0-7910-1663-3
      ISBN 0-7910-2028-2 (paper)
1. Kiowa Indians—Juvenile literature. I. Title. II. Series.        93-17696
E99.K5D65 1994                                                      CIP
973'.04974—dc20                                                     AC

# CONTENTS

*Kiowa artist George Silverhorn's watercolor* Woman on a Horse, *painted in 1966. Like most of the tribes of the Great Plains, the Kiowa were superb riders.*

# CHAPTER 1

# The Black Hills

In western South Dakota and eastern Wyoming, a group of mountains rise up darkly against the sky. Because of the dark pine trees that cover their slopes, these mountains appear to be almost black. They are known as the *Black Hills.* The Black Hills seem to spring up suddenly from the flat grasslands and prairie known as the *Great Plains.*

The Great Plains are like an ocean. Unless a person is far enough to the west to see the Black Hills or the Rocky Mountains beyond, the Great Plains stretch from horizon to horizon. They cover a major part of the central-western United States, including the states of Kansas, Oklahoma, Nebraska, North and South Dakota, Wyoming, Montana, and parts of Texas and New Mexico.

Toward the northwestern end of the Great Plains, the Black Hills appear. They rise up out of the flatlands like castles. Unlike the dry, sun-baked prairie, much of the Black Hills are cool and shadowy forest. Thick with trees, they are home to many forms of wild-life. Cold, clear streams are filled with trout and other fish. Families of deer linger among the pines. Rabbit and fowl are plentiful. The Black Hills are like an oasis rising from a massive desert of dust and grass.

For centuries, Native American Indian tribes of the Great Plains coveted the Black Hills. Compared to the harsh, thirsty Plains, the valleys of the Black Hills with their streams and woodlands provided an ideal place to set up a village. There was plenty of game for food, and shelter from the sun. And there were frequent rains to replenish the streams and cool off the midday heat in the summer months. In the winter, the val-leys sheltered tribes from the blizzards that howled across the Plains. But for the tribes of the Plains region, the Black Hills were more than just a comfortable place to live.

For the Indians of the Plains, the Black Hills were sacred. They were a kind of church, a holy place to be honored, worshiped, and protected. The hills represented the goodness of nature. The various tribes who lived there over the years all felt this way about the Black Hills. The tribes fought wars over possession of the hills. The modern-day Sioux, descendants of the last tribe to inhabit the Black Hills before the coming of the white man, still regard the Black Hills as sacred.

Among the earliest tribes to inhabit the Black Hills were the Kiowa. The term *Kiowa* refers to two closely related tribes that traveled and lived together—the Kiowa and the Kiowa-Apache.

During the early 17th century, these peoples came to the Black Hills from their original homelands in western Montana and southern Saskatchewan, Canada. It was there, according to Kiowa creation beliefs, that the first Kiowa man and woman emerged from a hollow cottonwood tree trunk. Europeans first saw them in the Black Hills in the 1700s. The white men described them as a tall, handsome, graceful people with proud, strong facial features. Their dark hair was so long that it sometimes reached the ground.

During their journey to the Black Hills, something happened that forever changed

A *buffalo skin painting of various supernatural figures from Kiowa legends. Among them are* Saynday, *the walking human figure, creater of the world.* Mankiah, *the whirlwind horse, flies on the upper right and also in front of* Saynday.

Kiowa *culture.* They obtained horses. Most likely, they were introduced to these animals by the Crow tribe, who lived near the Black Hills. Horses first came to the Great Plains with the Spanish explorers known as *conquistadores* in the 1500s. The Plains tribes first got hold of strays and then became expert at stealing the animals from the Spaniards—and from one another. Soon the Plains tribes were masterful horsemen themselves.

Horses played such an important role in Kiowa existence that the tribe eventually believed that they had created these animals. For how else could men become masters of such powerful, swift creatures? According to Kiowa legends, they made the first horse, but it was too powerful and wild to ride. This horse galloped off across the Plains to become *mankiah*—the whirlwind. But the Kiowa mastered its lesser offspring, which were made only partly of the whirlwind.

After settling in the Black Hills, the Kiowa, like the other Plains tribes, became bold and expert horsemen. They rode out from the Black Hills onto the Plains to hunt and do battle with rival tribes. Because they had created the whirlwind and mastered its offspring, the Kiowa never feared the great storms and tornadoes that often swept across the Great Plains. They made alliances with some neighboring tribes and drove away more hostile tribes who raided their lands. And so the Kiowa thrived as guardians of the sacred Black Hills. They were a strong people who feared little, and who were at one with their natural surroundings. ▲

*Buffalo Chase, drawn by Kiowa warrior Wo-haw. The Kiowa way of life depended on the buffalo herds that roamed the Great Plains.*

CHAPTER **2**

# Sun Dance

For tribes of the Great Plains such as the Kiowa, there was an animal that was just as important as the horse to their culture and day-to-day life. This was the buffalo. These shaggy beasts were so essential to Plains tribes that white men called these peoples buffalo Indians.

During the years of the 18th century that the Kiowa lived in and around the Black Hills, the buffalo thrived on the Great Plains. Great herds of buffalo thundered across the grasslands, kicking up clouds of dust that could be seen for miles. When the first Europeans

13

came to the Plains in the 16th century, they were astonished at the size of these herds. At that time, more than 60 million buffalo rumbled over the prairie. The largest herds covered areas the size of entire states such as Kansas. They were as "plentiful as fish in the sea," one Spaniard wrote.

By the time the Kiowa settled in the Black Hills, there were not quite so many buffalo. But there were still more than enough to support comfortably all the tribes of the central and northern Great Plains that depended on them. These tribes included the Kiowa, their neighbors to the north—the Crow, Arapaho, Mandan, Blackfoot, and Arikara—and other nearby tribes such as the Cheyenne, Hidatsa, Shoshone, and Comanche.

But the buffalo provided much more than just food for the Kiowa. They were at the center of the Kiowa way of life. The daily and seasonal cycles of Kiowa culture revolved around the buffalo. In fact, the very survival of the Plains tribes depended on these animals. The buffalo hunt, then, was a truly special event for the Kiowa.

Although the object of the hunt was to kill these animals, the Kiowa recognized that the buffalo allowed them to survive. And so the Kiowa respected the buffalo and regarded them as sacred. A buffalo hunt was preceded by religious rituals and ceremonies. In these ceremonies, the Kiowa both honored the buffalo and prayed for a successful hunt by dancing and singing. Kiowa religion involved various supernatural beings. The most important of these was *Saynday,* the creator of the world. The Kiowa also attached great spiritual significance to many aspects of nature, such as the sun and moon, corn and tobacco, certain animals, and to sacred places and objects. The spirit of nature itself was worshiped.

After the religious rituals, a hunting party armed with bows and arrows and lances would ride out across the Plains. The hunting parties were led by warriors known as *Dog Soldiers.* These men were among the finest members of the five Kiowa warrior societies. Young boys started out as members of the lowest warrior society—the Polanyup, or rabbits. The boys would try and work their way upward to the top warrior society—the Koitsenko. This was done through actions of bravery in battles with other tribes. For the Kiowa and many other tribes, the bravest deed in battle was to touch an enemy warrior but not to kill or harm him.

The buffalo brought back to the villages by the hunters were used in every possible way.

Their meat was eaten. Their hides were used for the tipis in which the Kiowa families lived, for the heavy robes worn during the winter, and for other types of clothing. Their bladders were fashioned into water carriers. Other inner organs were used as containers as well. Livers and brains were used in the process of softening the hides, and skulls were used as bowls. Buffalo bones were

*Kiowa women prepare buffalo hides for making clothing and tipis. The woman in the foreground scrapes fur from a hide. The woman in the background stretches another hide in preparation for the softening process.*

fashioned into tools and eating utensils. Tendons and sinews made a strong thread. Buffalo horns and hooves were ground into powders that would be used in medicines by Kiowa healers. Kiowa women were responsible for most of these tasks, such as making robes and tipis. Even the dung of the buffalo was put to good use. On a cold night out on the Plains, where firewood was scarce, Kiowa travelers would burn the dried buffalo chips for fuel.

The buffalo provided the Kiowa with food and the other materials required to maintain physical well-being. Kiowa social and spiritual needs were satisfied in a variety of ways. The tribe was divided into bands. The bands were extended groups of tribespeople who were usually related to one another. A band could have as few as 12 tipis or as many as 50, with each tipi housing a family. Each band had a chief. Usually, the chiefs were particularly brave warriors. They might also be men of great spiritual wisdom or power. The chiefs would hold councils to decide important tribal issues.

The Kiowa also might turn to other members of the tribe for spiritual guidance or other needs. Certain tribespeople had special powers. These men and women usually belonged to religious societies of one kind or another. A Kiowa who was ill or a warrior who was wounded in battle, for example, would seek out a member of the Buffalo Doctor Society. Members of this society had the power to cure and heal. Kiowas who wanted to know whether their marriage would be successful might turn to a member of the Owl Doctor Society. Owl Doctors had the power of prophesy. Those who had magical powers belonged to the Eagle Shield Society. Certain powerful older women belonged to the mysterious Bear Women Society. Songs, dancing, dream interpretations, visions brought about by fasting in sacred places, and rituals involving sacred objects were used by the members of these societies to achieve their goals.

One of the most important Kiowa societies was the Sun Dance Shield Society. The members of this group kept and guarded the most sacred object of the Kiowa tribe. This was the *tai-me.* The tai-me was a small green stone carved into the shape of a person. It was decorated with a robe of white feathers, an ermine skin, and a tobacco leaf as a headdress. The *Sun Dance*—the most essential of Kiowa spiritual rituals—revolved around the tai-me.

The Sun Dance was a celebration of life and a tribal prayer for the well-being of the

Kiowa Sun Dance, by
modern-day Kiowa artist
Sharron Ahtone. The
sacred tai-me is at the
bottom and to the left
of the center pole.

Kiowa. It took place once a year, usually in June. The sun, known as Pahy, was the focus of the ritual. The time and place of the dance would be announced each year by a member of the Sun Dance Shield Society. Then all the bands would gather at the chosen site. They would assemble their tipis in a great circle. In the center of the circle, a sacred lodge was built. The lodge was a round shelter constructed of cottonwood branches and 17 supporting poles. In the center of the Sun

Dance lodge was a pole. The tai-me was hung from this pole. The spiritual powers of the sun that the dancers hoped to attract would be transmitted through the tai-me to the dancers and the tribe.

The Sun Dance celebration began with a buffalo dance. Dressed in buffalo skins, the Kiowa imitated the sacred buffalo as they danced. Then, the young warriors who would participate in the actual Sun Dance entered the sacred lodge. The Sun Dance featured four days of dancing, singing, fasting, and other rituals involving the tai-me. A sun dancer might dance on behalf of himself, a friend, his band, or the entire tribe. He might dance for good fortune in hunting and battle, or for spiritual health and power. He might also dance for more specific things, such as the love of a woman or the recovery of a sick family member.

In the meantime, outside the lodge, the entire tribe held a great celebration. Gifts were given, games were played, old friendships were renewed, young people met and pledged marriage, and the bands and societies gave dinners. On the final night of the Sun Dance, a huge feast was held. The next morning, the ceremony ended. The sacred lodge was taken down. The tai-me was taken away by a member of the Sun Dance Shield Society, to be watched over until next year's celebration. Strengthened and renewed by the Sun Dance, the Kiowa returned to their day-to-day lives in the Black Hills and on the Great Plains. ◭

A Kiowa in battle; Black Legs Warrior, *by Roland Whitehorse. During the 1700s, the Kiowas' hold on the Black Hills was challenged by a number of hostile tribes. Their most powerful enemy was the Sioux Nation.*

CHAPTER **3**

# The Last Stand of the Cold Men

The Kiowa, compared to many of the other Plains peoples, were a small tribe. And yet, for almost a century, they held the most sought after land of the Great Plains—the Black Hills. This was no easy task. But the Kiowa were courageous warriors. They had strong allies in the large Crow Indian nation of Montana. They also enjoyed peaceful trade relations with the Mandan, Hidatsa, and Arikara tribes. These were agricultural peoples who lived along the upper Missouri

23

River. They traded the food products they grew for Kiowa buffalo skins.

But other tribes were not so friendly. Kiowa warriors were constantly on the alert for Comanche raiding parties. The Comanches were known as fierce fighters. They had a reputation as being the most expert and daring horsemen on the Great Plains. They also greatly outnumbered the Kiowa.

As the 1700s progressed, Kiowa warriors were forced regularly to ride out and drive off Comanche raiders. But the Comanches grew bolder and returned again and again. Their raiding parties grew larger and larger. By 1770, open warfare had broken out between the Kiowa and the Comanche. Young Kiowa warriors had plenty of chances to make their way upward through the Kiowa warrior societies.

The situation grew steadily worse for the Kiowa. Other tribes, feeling that the Kiowa were vulnerable, began to put pressure on the Black Hills. The Shoshone attacked them from the west. From the north came the Cheyenne and their allies, the Arapaho. And from the east came the greatest threat of all—the war parties of the Sioux Nation.

The Sioux Nation was huge and warlike. It included many different Sioux tribes. The three main Sioux groups were the Lakota

*In 1785, most of the Kiowa abandoned the Black Hills to the Sioux and their allies. A small group of courageous Kiowa warriors—known as the Cold Men—fought off the Sioux assault for 10 more years, but they too were eventually driven from the Black Hills. Stephen Mopope's* On the Move *portrays the Kiowas' exodus to the southern Great Plains.*

Sioux, the Dakota Sioux, and the Nakota Sioux. The Sioux were fearless in combat; they took great joy in battle and they outnumbered all their enemies. They also had a weapon that gave them an overwhelming advantage in battle—guns obtained from French traders. During open warfare on the Plains, lances, bows, and arrows could not compete with firearms.

During the 18th century, the Sioux had been moving steadily southward from North Dakota, Minnesota, and Canada. They overran the tribes that stood in their way, driving them away to the south. Even the fierce

Comanche were no match for the power of the Sioux. By the late 1700s, the Sioux controlled much of the northern Great Plains, and they were attacking tribes along the upper Missouri River. Now they set their sights on Kiowa lands. They began raiding Kiowa hunting grounds around the Black Hills.

The Kiowa found themselves cut off from their Crow allies and their trading partners on the upper Missouri River. They were under constant attack by the Dakota Sioux. To make matters worse, in 1781 a *smallpox* epidemic swept through the Kiowa settlements, reducing their strength even further. In 1785, the Kiowa chiefs held a council. Many of them wanted to abandon the Black Hills to the Sioux and retreat to the south. About one-third of them wanted to remain and fight.

The Kiowa tribe split up. The majority of the Kiowa bands headed south across the Plains, away from the fearful Sioux. The rest of them remained in the Black Hills. Those who remained were a hardened group of about 100 warriors and their families. They became known as the Cold Men because they remained in the colder north instead of heading south. And although they were badly outnumbered and outgunned by the Sioux and the Shoshone, they fought for the sacred Black Hills with desperate bravery.

The Cold Men, against all odds, held the Black Hills for 10 years. They thrashed the Shoshone repeatedly in battle, and formed a brief alliance with the Arapaho and Cheyenne, who were also under attack by the Sioux. Soon, however, these tribes formed alliances with the Sioux. The Crow held their ground in Montana, but they could offer little help to the Kiowa.

By 1795, the Cold Men were starving. The Sioux had pinned them in the Black Hills and taken control of Kiowa hunting grounds. In a final battle with the Sioux, the Kiowa were badly defeated. They had no choice but to abandon the Black Hills or be wiped out or enslaved. The Kiowa who still survived set out to the south to find the rest of their tribe. They left the beloved Black Hills behind them forever. The sacred hills belonged to the Sioux now. ▲

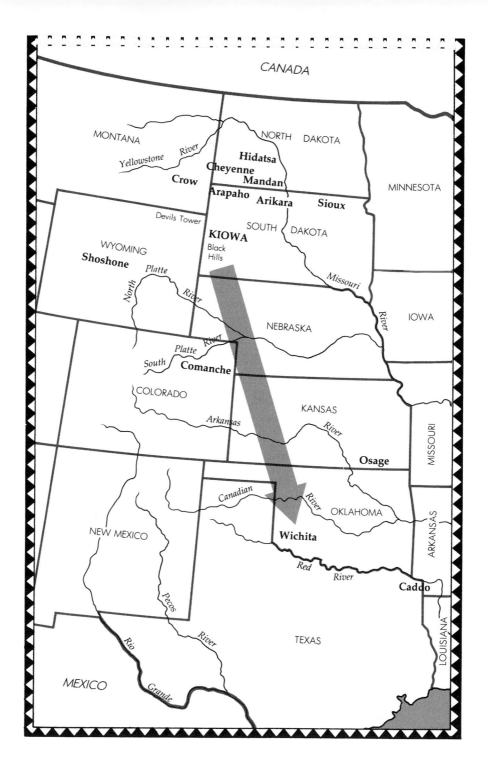

CHAPTER **4**

# The Kiowa Reunited

**W**hile the Northern Kiowa were holding out in the Black Hills, the rest of the tribe was engaged in an exodus that eventually brought them as far south as New Mexico. They became known as the Southern Kiowa. For the Southern Kiowa, life was much different than it had been on the bountiful northern Plains and in the Black Hills. The New Mexico territory was harsh and unforgiving. Food, especially buffalo, was harder to come by.

And the Southern Kiowa began to encounter members of a strange new tribe. These newcomers were white. They had hair on their face. Many of them were medicine men—Spanish Roman Catholic missionaries—who preached a new kind of religion. They tried to persuade the Kiowa and the other tribes of the south to accept this new religion. But the Kiowa preferred the Sun Dance and their own rituals. There were other white men, however, who had come to settle and trade with the Indians. These white men had many horses, guns, food, and other goods.

One day a party of Southern Kiowa visited a Spanish settlement in New Mexico to trade

*The Kiowa encountered Catholic missionaries in the Southwest, as depicted here in Kiowa painter Jack Hokeah's mural* Father Ricklin . . . in Council with Chiefs.

with the Spaniards. At the settlement, the Kiowa met a group of Comanches, their traditional enemies from the northern Plains. The Comanche tribe had also been driven south by the Sioux. The two old enemies confronted one another, ready to resume their hostilities. But some of the Spaniards stepped between the two parties and acted as peacemakers. They convinced the Southern Kiowas and the Comanches to sit together and talk.

Guikate, the leader of the Southern Kiowa band, spoke first. He said that his people had no wish for war with the Comanche. He told of how his people had been driven from their homeland by the Sioux and had left behind many of their best fighters. They had made a long, hard journey that lasted for many years. His people had suffered much sadness and many hardships along the way. And although they had no fear of the Comanche, war would not be a good thing for either tribe.

Pareiyi, the leader of the Comanche band, agreed. His people too had suffered at the hands of the Sioux. But although Pareiyi also wanted peace between the Kiowa and the Comanche, he was not a powerful enough leader to speak for his entire tribe. He invited

Guikate to come with him. They would journey among the Comanche bands and discuss the issue. Guikate agreed to go with the Comanche. But he warned Pareiyi that if he had not returned safely to his own people within a year, the Southern Kiowa would avenge his death.

Guikate traveled with Pareiyi for a year. The two former enemies visited many Comanche bands and camps throughout parts of New Mexico, Arkansas, Texas, and Oklahoma. Guikate accompanied the ferocious Comanche on raids of other tribes. They also attacked white settlements, where horses, guns, food, and prisoners were taken. During his time with the Comanche, Guikate was treated with honor and respect. After a year, he returned to his own people in New Mexico to report on what he had seen.

As a result of the year that Guikate spent among the Comanche, the two tribes formed an alliance. Together, the Southern Kiowa and the Comanche were a powerful force on the southern Plains. They shared the same hunting grounds. And they went out on raids together, ranging far and wide. Soon they were the terror of the southern Plains. White settlers and other tribes feared them.

*continued on page 41*

# PAINTERS OF THE PLAINS

Art has always been an essential aspect of traditional Kiowa culture. Buffalo-hide picture calenders record the history of the tribe, from day-to-day tribal life to events of special importance. The Kiowa used paintings and drawings to depict their inner spiritual life, dreams, visions, tribal legends, and supernatural beings as well. Kiowa leaders used paintings to signify their stature, and the different tribal societies were identified through painted symbols. Shields, tipis, clothing, weapons, and other implements were painted decoratively.

Originally, Kiowa artists used ground up, colored rocks and soil mixed with water as paint. Later, they learned to use modern instruments and techniques. In the 1920s, five young Kiowas—who came to be known as the Kiowa Five—studied at the University of Oklahoma School of Art. These young artists painted scenes of traditional Kiowa life. In doing so, they helped to revive the fading Kiowa culture. Art, which came naturally to the Kiowa, was never so important to the tribe as it was then. Today, Kiowa art and artists continue to flourish. The style of Kiowa art grows more modern with the times, but the subject—traditional Kiowa culture—remains the focus.

*A headdress or bonnet case of rawhide, painted with a geometric design.*

Drawing of the Sun Dance, made in a notebook by a Kiowa warrior named Wo-haw, who was imprisoned at Fort Marion in the 1870s.

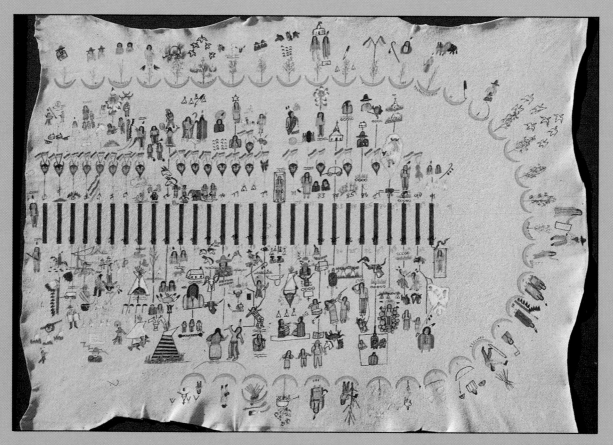

The buffalo-hide calendar drawn by Anko around 1864 to 1893. In the 1890s, Anko recreated his calendar in pencil on brown paper at the request of ethnologist James Mooney.

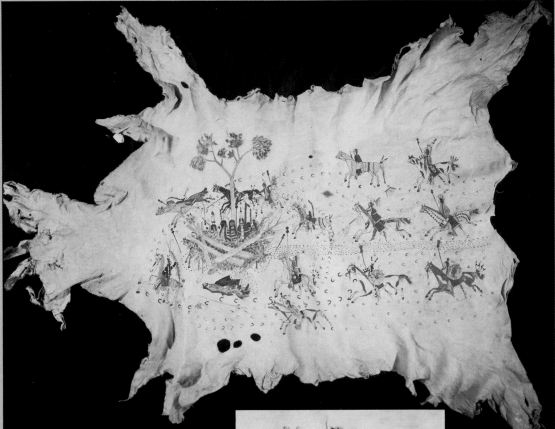

Sun Dance: The Sham Battle, painted by Silverhorn in the late 19th century. Silverhorn was a leader of the Sun Dance ritual as well as an artist; he was also the uncle and first art teacher of Kiowa Five painter Stephen Mopope.

*Detail from* Sun Dance.

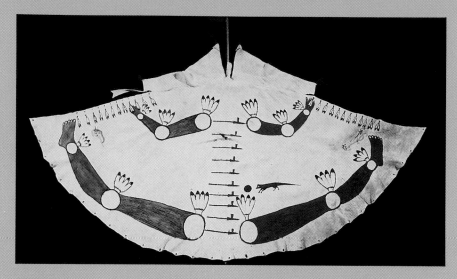

The unusual Leg-Picture Tipi captures a vision seen by Fair-Haired Old Man. The disembodied legs and arms are adorned by feathers.

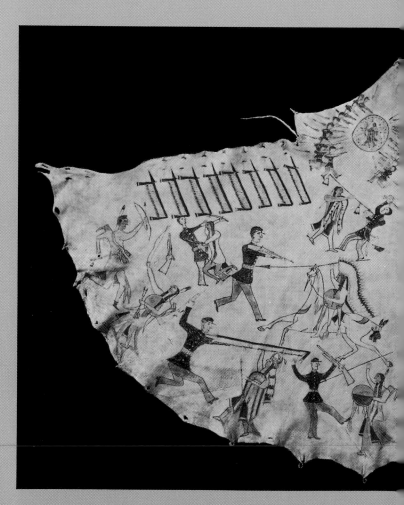

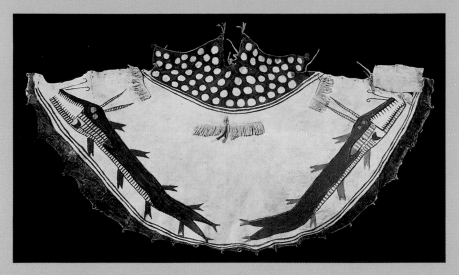

*Underwater-Monster Tipi. According to Kiowa legend, the horned fish, or Zemoguani, might lurk in caverns to kill a swimmer.*

*The Battle-Picture Tipi of Little Bluff, the Kiowa principal chief who died in 1866. The painting records courageous acts by several Kiowa against enemy warriors and U.S. soldiers.*

The Kiowa Five painted scenes of their people's history and experience. Asah, Hokeah, and Mopope were dancers; Aukiah and Tsatoke were singers and drummers. They were concerned with perpetuating Kiowa traditions in all of the arts.

*Stephen Mopope's* Indian Dancer.

*Jack Hokeah's* Chasing Evil Spirits.

*Lois (Bou-ge-tah) Smokey's* Kiowa Family.

*Monroe Tsatoke's* Dance of the Dog Soldiers.

Tribal Memories, *by Robert Redbird (born 1939), incorporates the fan of the peyote ritual with dreamlike images of the buffalo and eagle. A new generation continues the Kiowa's artistic traditions.*

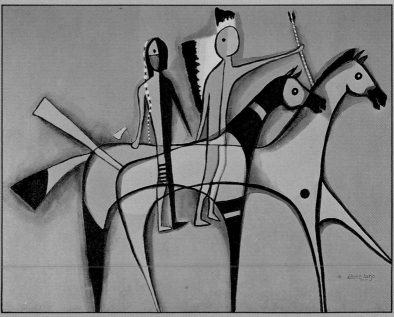

*Sharron Ahtone Harjo's* Return Them Safely to Home, *a 1971 work in acrylic on canvas, commemorates a historic event of the 1860s, in which Kiowa warriors captured a prized possession—a beaded lance—of an enemy tribe.*

*continued from page 32*

By 1790, the Kiowa-Comanche alliance had taken control of the entire southern Plains region. They drove the Tonkawa tribe off the Plains and into central Texas. They forced the Wichita tribe of Kansas to flee eastward across the Wichita Mountains into Oklahoma. Even the fierce Apache bands were forced to retreat from Kansas and northern New Mexico to southern New Mexico and then across the border into Mexico. White settlers and missionaries entered Kiowa-Comanche territory at their own risk.

While the Southern Kiowa and their Comanche allies were becoming the dominant force on the southern Plains, the Northern Kiowa were moving ever southward in search of their long-lost tribe. They apparently halted in Nebraska for a period, setting up camp on the North Platte River. The Sioux continued to menace them. The last of the Cold Men attempted to reach the Missouri River to barter for horses and guns with British traders. Eventually they moved on again, heading south, questioning hopefully any friendly Indians or white people they encountered about the whereabouts of their tribe.

Finally, around 1806, the Northern Kiowa reached New Mexico and were reunited with

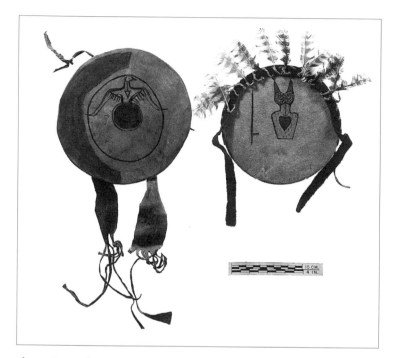

*Shields painted with the symbols of the Kiowa Eagle Shield (left) and Owl Doctor (right) societies. In 1806, the Northern and Southern Kiowa were finally reunited; the fragmented religious societies regained their power, and the Kiowa tribe was whole once again.*

the Southern Kiowa. It was an occasion of great happiness, for the tribe had been separated for 20 years. The Southern Kiowa rejoiced to see the long-lost part of their tribe that had refused to leave the Black Hills. The Northern Kiowa were amazed to see that their tribe had become allied with the Comanche, and that the two former mortal enemies had become lords of the southern Plains. The arrival of the Northern Kiowa only made the Kiowa-Comanche alliance stronger.

After 20 years, the Kiowa were whole again. They were as proud and strong as ever. Their allies were the most feared warriors in the land. But in the times to come, the strength of the Kiowa would be tested to the utmost. Soon their society and their very way of life would be threatened with destruction. ▲

CHAPTER **5**

# "She Saw the Last Buffalo Herd"

The Kiowa probably first encountered white men in the late 1700s. The Southern Kiowa, who had recently arrived in New Mexico, occasionally made contact with Spanish traders and missionaries. British and French fur trappers and traders, despite the threat of the Sioux, made their way up the Missouri River and ventured out onto the Plains. There, they bartered with Plains

*Chief Dohasan's picture of the terrifying Cut-Throat Massacre— suffered by a band of Kiowa at the hands of the Osage tribe— recorded in the chief's calendar of Kiowa history.*

tribes, exchanging guns, liquor, and metal knives and hatchets for horses and buffalo hides. The Europeans brought something else with them as well, which they passed on to the Plains Indians for free—disease. Smallpox and *cholera* epidemics, contracted from the Europeans by the Indians, devastated the tribes.

More threatening to the Kiowa and the other Plains tribes was the growing number of white Americans moving into and across Indian territory. The United States frontier was expanding steadily westward during the first decades of the 1800s. Homesteaders, buffalo hunters, traders, and men simply looking for adventure were becoming a common sight on the southern Great Plains.

Some of these newcomers passed through and continued westward. Others, however, made it clear that they intended to settle on the Plains and start new lives there. They established ranches and farms. They brought wives and children and dogs and livestock. They built fences and let their cattle graze on the grasslands or plowed up great patches of grassland for farming. And they began to slaughter the buffalo.

Many of the white people killed the buffalo because their cattle needed the grasslands for grazing, just as the buffalo herds needed the same grasslands to survive. It was a matter of competition for a food source between the cattle and the buffalo. Later, as the railroads came through Indian lands, the buffalo were killed to make room for the tracks. Other white men killed the buffalo for sport. These men made names for themselves as "great buffalo hunters" by riding among the herds and slaughtering them with rifles. They killed the buffalo by the thousands and left the corpses to rot in the sun.

The Indians could not understand such behavior. Why would a man kill more buffalo than he could eat or use for trading purposes? The Indians watched in disgust and with growing alarm, for *they* needed the buffalo to survive. Many of the tribes, and especially the Comanche, Kiowa, Cheyenne, and Apache, stepped up their attacks on the wagon trains and settlements. In order to protect its citizens, the U.S. government began building forts on the frontier.

Although they were weakened by epidemics and the dwindling buffalo herds, the Kiowa and their Comanche allies maintained their grip on the southern Plains. War was now a way of life for the Kiowa. They had become a great warrior tribe; they

*A Kiowa drawing of the ravages of smallpox. Cholera and smallpox epidemics repeatedly devastated the tribes of the Great Plains.*

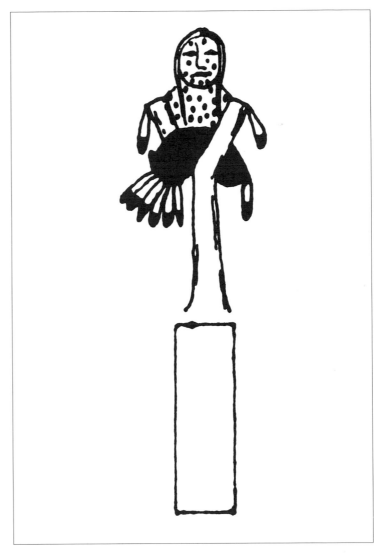

were raiders and conquerors like the Sioux and Comanche. They still battled occasionally with the Sioux, but that powerful tribe for the most part stayed to the north and on the upper Missouri River. Now the enemies of the Kiowa were the Osage, Pawnee, Cheyenne, Wichita, Fox, and Sac tribes. And, along with the Comanche, they continued their raids on white travelers and homesteaders. But the period of Kiowa dominance on the southern Great Plains was coming to an end. In 1833, the Cut-Throat Massacre, a tragic day in Kiowa history, occurred.

One day during the summer of 1833, the Kiowa chief A'date, leader of all the Kiowa bands, led a party of Kiowa into the Wichita Mountains in Kansas. While the Kiowa men were out searching for food, a war party of Osage attacked their unprotected camp. The Osage massacred all the women, children, and elders in the camp. They cut off their heads and left them in kettles for the Kiowa warriors to find when they returned. The Osage also stole the sacred tai-me, which was under the protection of a member of the Kiowa party. Chief A'date fell into disgrace for allowing the slaughter to occur. He was replaced by Chief Dohasan, who would lead the Kiowa for 30 years.

The Kiowa would remember that summer as "The Summer That They Cut Off Our Heads." It resulted in a feud between the Kiowa and the Osage that lasted until 1836, when the Osage returned the tai-me, allowing the Kiowa to hold their first Sun Dance in years. A more fateful occurrence came about because of the Cut-Throat Massacre, however. This was the appearance of soldiers of the United States Army.

During the summer that followed the Cut-Throat Massacre, a troop of U.S. Cavalry rode into the Kiowa camp. Their mission was apparently peaceful and friendly. With them they had a young Kiowa girl who had been kidnapped by the Osage during the Cut-Throat Massacre. They returned the girl to the tribe. Then they asked the Kiowa to attend a peace conference at Fort Gibson in Oklahoma. The U.S. government wanted to put a stop to the wars between the Plains tribes, the leader of the cavalry troop said. But more important to the government was convincing the tribes to halt their attacks on settlers and wagon trains.

Because the white "horse soldiers" had returned the kidnapped Kiowa girl and treated the Kiowa with respect, the Kiowa agreed to attend the conference at Fort Gibson. But many of the Kiowa, including Chief Dohasan, sensed that the arrival of U.S. troops in their camp signaled dark days to come.

The Kiowa sent representatives to the peace conference at Fort Gibson. It was held

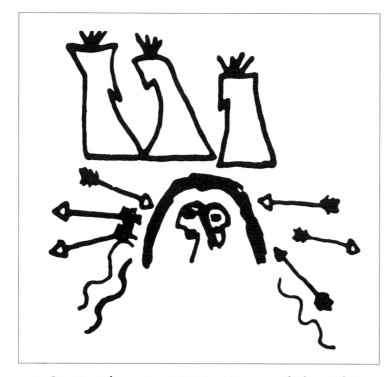

*A drawing in Chief Dohasan's calendar representing a battle between the Kiowa and the Cheyenne in 1838. Soon after, however, the two tribes joined forces in the war against white invaders of their territory.*

on September 2, 1834. Many of the Plains tribes attended. Most of the tribes agreed to a peace treaty between themselves, the United States, Mexico, and the Republic of Texas, which was not yet part of the United States. But the Kiowa refused to sign and left the conference early. The Kiowa resistance had officially begun.

In 1837, the U.S. government persuaded the Kiowa to attend another meeting at Fort Gibson by bribing the tribe with trade goods and other gifts. Ten lesser Kiowa chiefs signed a treaty with the United States. But

Principal Chief Dohasan did not sign. The Kiowa continued their raids on farms and ranches in Texas and New Mexico. In 1940, the Kiowa-Comanche alliance was joined by the Cheyenne and Arapaho tribes. The warriors of these four tribes targeted the Santa Fe Trail, the primary trade route between Independence, Missouri, and Santa Fe, New Mexico. Wagon trains loaded with goods were attacked. Soon, word spread that it was not safe for white travelers to use the trail. Even large escorts of U.S. Cavalry troops and the famed Texas Rangers, who were expert Indian fighters, could not protect the caravans from the Indian raids.

Unable to protect the Santa Fe Trail, the U.S. government attempted to buy off the Indians. In 1853, a group of Kiowa and Comanche chiefs signed a treaty at Fort Atkinson, Oklahoma. The Indians were offered a total of $18,000 in cash and trade goods if they would end their attacks on the Santa Fe Trail and allow roads to be built through their territory. Again, a group of minor chiefs signed, but Dohasan did not. The raids continued. Chief Dohasan openly defied the U.S. government. "The white chief is a fool," Dohasan said. "He is a coward. His heart is small—not larger than a pebble. His men are

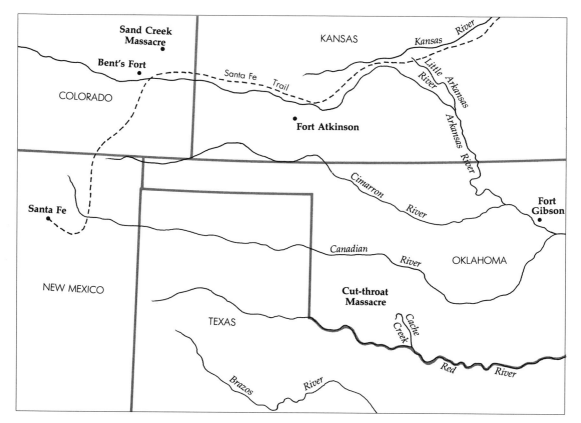

not strong—too few to contend with my warriors."

Despite Chief Dohasan's defiance, the southern Great Plains were steadily slipping from the grasp of the Kiowa and the other tribes. Their way of life was dying. Year by year, more white people came. To the Indians, it seemed like a great pale flood. In 1858, thousands upon thousands of hopeful gold miners poured through Kiowa territory on their way west to California during the gold rush. The buffalo herds were disappear-

*Kiowa-Comanche territory at the time of the Cut-Throat Massacre in 1833. The Sand Creek Massacre in Colorado (upper left) left hundreds of unarmed Cheyenne women, children, and elderly slaughtered by Colorado state forces. The massacre enraged tribes across the Great Plains.*

ing. The Kiowa suffered through "antelope winters," when there was no buffalo meat to be eaten and the tribe was forced to hunt antelope and even jackrabbit to survive. They froze through the brutal Plains winters because of a lack of buffalo robes. And epidemics of smallpox and cholera continued to ravage the tribe.

The Kiowa fought on, but they were severely weakened by the long winters of cold, hunger, and disease. Now they suffered one crushing defeat after another. With the American Civil War ending, white soldiers and Indian fighters such as Kit Carson arrived in force. They distributed deadly new carbine repeating rifles to the Kiowa's Indian enemies, such as the Sac and Fox tribes. The Kiowa, who had few guns of any kind, lost many of their bravest warriors in battle. Their encampments and villages were attacked and burned.

And the buffalo seemed to have vanished completely. For the Kiowa, this meant that the end of the world must be coming. According to Old Lady Horse, a Kiowa wise woman, the few surviving buffalo had gone to live inside sacred Mount Scott in Oklahoma.

"The buffalo were the life of the Kiowas," Old Lady Horse said. "So, when the white men wanted to build railroads, or when they wanted to farm or raise cattle, the buffalo still protected the Kiowas. They tore up the railroad tracks and the gardens. They chased the cattle off the ranges. The buffalo loved the Kiowas as much as the Kiowas loved them. . . . Then the white men hired hunters to do nothing but kill the buffalo. Up and down the plains those men ranged, shooting sometimes as many as a hundred buffalo a day.

"The buffalo saw that their day was over. They could protect the Kiowas no longer. Sadly, the last remnant of the great herd gathered in council and decided what they would do.

"The Kiowas were camped on the north side of Mount Scott. One young woman got up very early in the morning. The dawn mist was still rising from Medicine Creek, and as she looked across the water, peering through the haze, she saw the last buffalo herd appear like a spirit dream.

"Straight to Mount Scott the leader of the herd walked. Behind him came the cows and their calves, and the few young males who had survived. As the woman watched, the face of the mountain opened.

"Inside Mount Scott the world was fresh and green, as it had been when she was a little girl. The rivers ran clear, not red. The wild plums were in blossom, chasing the red buds up the inside slopes. Into this world of beauty the buffalo walked, never to be seen again." ▲

CHAPTER **6**

# The Last Sun Dance

Late in 1865, the demoralized Kiowa signed the Little Arkansas Treaty. They agreed to live on a government *reservation* in western Oklahoma and Texas. They would stay within the boundaries of the reservation and halt their war against the United States. They would be given food, blankets, shelter, and other goods by the government. This time, Principal Chief Dohasan signed the treaty. He died soon after on the reservation.

The Kiowa did not react well to reservation life. There were no buffalo to hunt, and the government did not supply them with the food and other goods they had promised. A new Kiowa chief, Satanta, led raiding parties off the reservation. Linking up with Comanche bands, the Kiowa attacked targets in central Texas. But the Indians soon learned that they were now up against an overpowering enemy.

Two great white warriors—General Philip Sheridan and General William Tecumseh Sherman—were now determined to crush the Indian resistance. These were hard, tough men who had played major roles in the Union defeat of the Confederacy in the bloody Civil War. They commanded armies the size of which the Kiowa had never imagined.

Sherman and Sheridan launched a major campaign against the Kiowa and the other Plains tribes who had refused to be confined to reservations. By 1874, armed Kiowa resistance had been stamped out. Chief Satanta was arrested and imprisoned in Texas. He died there several years later. As the winter of 1874 arrived, the remaining Kiowa warriors were freezing and near starvation, their horses killed or rounded up by the U.S. Army.

*The death of Chief Dohasan in 1866, recorded in a Kiowa calendar. The owl represents death. The wagon represents one that belonged to the chief and that was traditionally associated with him.*

One by one or in small groups they made their way to Fort Sill on the Oklahoma reservation and surrendered. Like the buffalo that had left the Great Plains and gone to live in sacred Mount Scott, it seemed that the day of the Kiowa was over.

For the Kiowa, however, there was no magical mountain of beauty for the tribe to disappear into. There was only the world of the white man. Now that the Kiowa had been broken militarily, the U.S. government began to break them culturally. It was decided in Washington, D.C., that the Kiowa would be better off—and would present less of a problem to white America—if they gave up their traditional ways and learned to exist as white people. A process of *assimilation* was begun on reservations across America.

For the Kiowa and other Native American tribes, assimilation seemed like a cultural death. Kiowa children were sent away to schools where they were isolated from the traditional ways of the tribe. Their long hair was cut short. They were discouraged from speaking their own language and made to wear white people's clothing and to adopt white people's manners. They were taught the history and heritage of Europeans and white Americans, while their own were ig-

nored. The boys were taught farming and the girls were taught how to be good housewives and secretaries.

The most fundamental assault on Kiowa culture was the prohibition of many of the Kiowa's spiritual rituals and ceremonies. Catholic priests attempted to persuade the Kiowa to forget their traditional religious practices and to become Catholics. In the summer of 1887, the Kiowa held a Sun Dance on the reservation at Oak Creek. The Oak Creek Sun Dance was the last Sun Dance held by the Kiowa. The following year,

*Defeated, starving, and freezing, the Kiowa straggle back to the Oklahoma reservation in the winter of 1874. The painting, Kiowa Submission, is by Kiowa artist Robert Redbird.*

Catholic priests on the reservation persuaded the government to declare the Sun Dance illegal.

The policy of *allotment* was another blow to Kiowa culture and pride. In 1887, a law was passed that divided the reservation into separate units of 160 acres. Each of these parcels of land was allotted, or granted, to a Kiowa and his family. The remainder—470,000 acres—was sold by the government to white settlers, ranchers, railroad companies, logging companies, and oil companies. The money received for these lands—$4 million—was put in a fund to be managed for the Kiowa by the government. But the Kiowa themselves saw little of this money.

By the turn of the century, it appeared that Kiowa culture was on the brink of extinction. The Kiowa, who had been one of the most powerful tribes of the Great Plains, seemed to be fading like ghosts. Their horse warriors once freely ranged across the southern Plains from New Mexico to Oklahoma and from Texas to Colorado. Their bands followed the great buffalo herds over thousands of miles of land that was known far and wide as Kiowa territory. They held the Sun Dance in the summer and had plenty of buffalo meat and buffalo robes in the winter.

A representation in a Kiowa calendar of the last Sun Dance, held at Oak Creek in the summer of 1887—a bitter moment in Kiowa history.

They danced the buffalo dance and told tales around the fire of Saynday and the whirlwind.

Now there was no more Sun Dance. There were no warrior societies to protect Kiowa land or religious societies to strengthen the Kiowa spirit. There were no chiefs to speak for their needs. The power of the sacred tai-me was broken. Where were the members of the magical Eagle Shield Society or the mysterious Bear Women Society now?

They were failed farmers and housewives who tended flimsy shacks.

With the allotment and the carving up of the reservations, government assistance became almost nonexistent. By the 1920s, the Kiowa had fallen into a state of rural and cultural poverty. Their efforts at farming and ranching were unsuccessful. Starvation and disease ravaged what was left of the Kiowa population. They froze through the winters in cheap housing with few blankets and barely enough to eat.

During the hot, dry Oklahoma summers, the Kiowa men stood at the edge of their dusty parcels of land. They leaned on the rakes and hoes given to them by the government years ago in an attempt to make farmers out of hunters and warriors. Their eyes searched the prairie and they listened to the empty wind. ▲

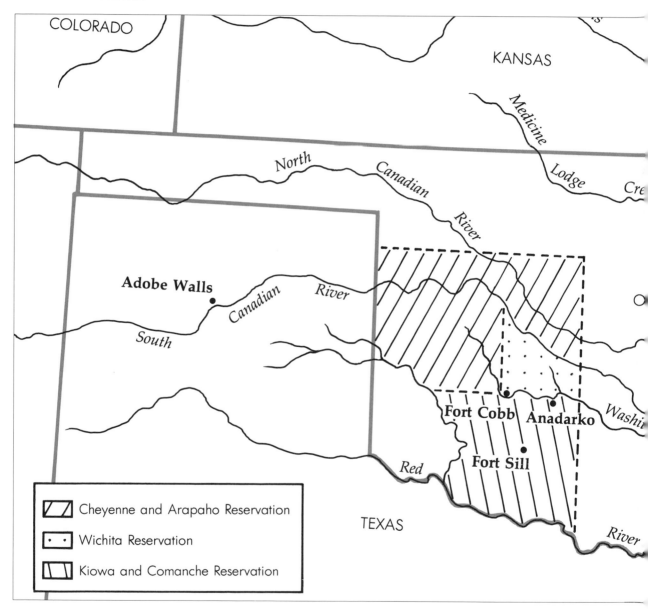

The Kiowa-Comanche reservation in Oklahoma, adjoined by the Wichita, Arapaho, and Cheyenne reservations.

COLORADO

KANSAS

Medicine

Lodge

Cre

North

Canadian

River

**Adobe Walls**

South

Canadian

River

Fort Cobb

Anadarko

Washi

**Fort Sill**

Red

River

TEXAS

Cheyenne and Arapaho Reservation

Wichita Reservation

Kiowa and Comanche Reservation

CHAPTER **7**

# The Seven Sisters in the Sky

The outer, natural world, where the Kiowa once thrived, no longer held a place for them. And so, in order to survive as a culture, the Kiowa turned elsewhere. The last buffalo herd had disappeared into Mount Scott, a place where no white men could follow. Now the Kiowa found their own Mount Scott. They found it within themselves. And there, they

OMA

river

discovered that the spirit of the Kiowa still lived.

The Kiowa had always been a deeply spiritual people. Their religious rituals, songs, and prayers provided them with an inner strength, both as a community and as individuals. Faced with the destruction of their culture, they once again found strength through religion. Because their own traditional religious rituals, such as the Sun Dance, had been banned, the Kiowa began to follow other spiritual paths. These paths led to the inner fortitude they needed to survive as a people.

The *Native American Church* was the spiritual route taken by many Kiowas in the late 19th and early 20th centuries. The Native American Church has its origins among Mexico's Indian tribes. It was eventually embraced by many of the Plains Indians, and it is still participated in today. The peyote ritual is the most important aspect of worship in the Native American Church. During this ceremony, members of the church ingest peyote, which comes from a cactus found in the American Southwest. The peyote allows worshipers to experience dreams and visions that put them in touch with their spiritual origins as Native Americans.

The Kiowa practice a peyote ritual known as the Little Moon ceremony. It lasts all night and includes prayers, songs, symbols, and ceremonial objects such as an eagle-feather fan, an eagle bone whistle, and a gourd rattle. Water is consumed at certain ritual moments throughout the night. As with the Sun Dance, during the Little Moon ceremony the participants pray for the well-being of the tribe.

Traditionally, another source of inner strength for the Kiowa had been art. The tribe's history, dating back to the time they inhabited the Black Hills, was recorded in pictures. Clothing, tipis, shields, lances, and buffalo skins were also used as canvases for Kiowa art. In the 1920s, five young Kiowa artists—Monroe Tsatoke, Stephen Mopope, Spencer Asah, James Auchiah, and Jack Hokeah—revived the custom of Kiowa art.

Admitted to the art school at the University of Oklahoma, these young men painted traditional Kiowa themes. Known as the Kiowa Five—and later, with the addition of Lois (Bou-ge-tah) Smokey, as the Kiowa Six—they inspired other Kiowa artists to use their talents to express the modern Native American experience and

*A Kiowa painting of a peyote ritual. The use of peyote to induce a spiritual state of mind is an important aspect of worship in the Native American Church.*

also to preserve traditional Native American culture in drawings and paintings. This practice is carried on today by Kiowa artists such as Robert Redbird and Sharron Ahtone Harjo. Kiowa sculptors and writers, such as the award-winning novelist and poet N. Scott Momaday, have also used their gifts to express and preserve the Kiowa experience.

Religion and art allowed the Kiowa to celebrate their own culture. It also gave many of them a feeling of cultural stability, which enabled them to deal more successfully with the overwhelming onslaught of white American culture. Many Kiowas fought in World War II, under the same flag that the troops of generals Sheridan and Sherman carried during the final campaign against the Kiowa warriors. Returning from the war, the veterans revived the old warrior societies. In this way, some Kiowas used a nontribal experience to help revive valuable traditions that had been neglected for decades. Other Kiowas began attending high schools and colleges and using their education to help their tribe. Kiowas who attended law schools, for example, often returned to Oklahoma and used what they learned to defend Kiowa rights under the law.

During the 1950s, 1960s, and 1970s, many young Kiowas left Oklahoma and traveled to cities such as Dallas, San Francisco, and Los Angeles to attend colleges and start businesses. They were encouraged by business grants and scholarships provided by the government. Some of them participated in the Korean War and the Vietnam War. But many of them struggled with their cultural identity. Could a Kiowa fight as an American soldier, or become a lawyer or a businessman in white society, and still feel like a true Kiowa?

Kiowa novelist and college professor N. Scott Momaday writes that "it's a matter of identity. It's thinking about who I am. I grew up on Indian reservations, and then I went away from the Indian world. But I continue to think of myself as an Indian."

Perry Horse, a Kiowa painter living in Washington, D.C., put it this way: "I think of myself as a Kiowa first, and an American citizen second."

Clearly, the Kiowa tribe is still staggering under the blow dealt to its identity and well-being by a vastly alien and overwhelming culture. Today, many of the Kiowa communities in Oklahoma are plagued by poor education, scarce employment opportunities, insufficient health care, and poverty.

*Al Momaday's drawing of Devils Tower in eastern Wyoming. According to tribal legends, a Kiowa boy was transformed into a bear (lower right), which attacked its seven sisters, who were saved when a tree stump they climbed onto grew into Devils Tower and hurled the seven sisters into the sky, where they became the seven stars of the Big Dipper constellation.*

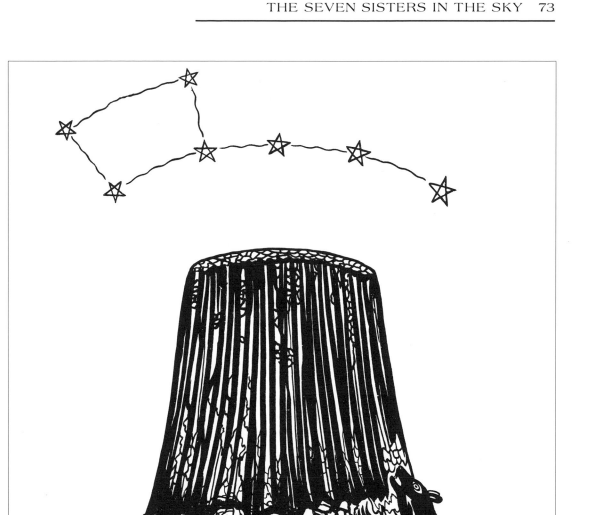

And yet, the Kiowa have survived. Back in the Black Hills country of Wyoming, there is an eerie-looking volcanic plateau with steep walls known as Devils Tower. It rises, stark and solitary, from the Wyoming grasslands. According to traditional Kiowa beliefs, one day long ago, eight Kiowa children—a brother and his seven sisters—were playing at the place where the Devils Tower now stands. Suddenly, the boy began to tremble. Then he turned into a ferocious grizzly bear. The seven sisters hid behind a large tree stump, for their brother clearly intended to eat them.

The tree stump spoke to the seven sisters, telling them to climb onto it. Then the stump began to grow, rising straight up toward the sky with the sisters on top. The angry bear clawed the sides of the magically rising tree stump, but soon the sisters were out of reach as the stump continued to rise. Finally, the towering stump hurled the seven sisters up into the sky. There, they were transformed into the seven stars of the Big Dipper constellation. The Kiowa believe to this day that the seven star sisters watch over them from their place in the sky. Even in the tribe's worst moments, a Kiowa has only to look up at the night sky to be assured that the seven Kiowa sisters are still there, shining down on them and protecting them. And until the day that the seven sisters fall from the sky, the Kiowa will survive. ▲

# CHRONOLOGY

**ca. 1640**   Kiowa migrate from original homelands in western Montana and southern Saskatchewan, Canada, to Black Hills region of South Dakota.

**ca. 1650**   Kiowa obtain horses from Crow tribe and form trade alliances with the Mandan, Hidatsa, and Arikara tribes.

**ca. 1770**   Kiowa battle Comanches; come under attack by the Shoshone, Arapaho, Cheyenne, and Sioux.

**1781**   Besieged by the Sioux, the Kiowa tribe separates. Most of the tribe flees south across the Plains, eventually arriving in New Mexico; the rest remain to defend the Black Hills.

**1790**   Southern Kiowa form an alliance with the Comanche and take control of a large portion of the southern Great Plains.

**1795**   Remaining Northern Kiowa are driven from the Black Hills by the Sioux. The survivors begin a long journey in search of the Southern Kiowa.

**1806**   Southern and Northern Kiowa are reunited in New Mexico. The Kiowa-Comanche alliance wages war against white homesteaders.

**1833**   Cut-Throat Massacre occurs. Kiowa encounter U.S. soldiers for the first time.

**ca. 1840**   Powerful Kiowa, Comanche, Cheyenne, and Arapaho alliance attacks Santa Fe Trail and wages open war against United States.

**1865**   Kiowa sign Little Arkansas Treaty and retire to Oklahoma reservation.

**1875**   Last Kiowa uprising is crushed by U.S. troops. Kiowa surrender and return to reservation.

**1887**   Last Kiowa Sun Dance is held. Assimilation and allotment policies are instituted. Kiowa traditional culture wanes.

**ca. 1900**   Many Kiowa embrace the Native American Church.

**ca. 1930**   Kiowa Six artists begin revival of Kiowa culture.

**1966**   Kiowa writer N. Scott Momaday receives Pulitzer Prize for his novel *House Made of Dawn*.

# GLOSSARY

| | |
|---|---|
| **allotment** | the division of reservation lands into privately owned tracts |
| **assimilation** | the process by which one culture absorbs another |
| **Black Hills** | a group of forested hills and mountains in western South Dakota and northeast Wyoming |
| **cholera** | a highly contagious intestinal disease caused by a bacterial infection |
| **conquistadores** | Sixteenth-century Spanish warrior-adventurers who explored and conquered Mexico and much of Central and South America |
| **culture** | the traditions, art, spiritual beliefs, language, and way of life of a people |
| **Dog Soldiers** | a term used by many Plains tribes for a group of elite warriors |
| **Great Plains** | a vast region of prairie and grasslands blanketing central North America |
| **mankiah** | in traditional Kiowa beliefs, the first horse, which was created by the Kiowa but was too powerful to ride and which galloped off across the plains to become the whirlwind |
| **Native American Church** | a religion embraced by many of the tribes of Mexico and the American southwest |
| **reservation** | an area of land with boundaries determined by the government, within which Indian tribes were forcibly settled |
| **Saynday** | in traditional Kiowa beliefs, the creator of the world |
| **smallpox** | a highly contagious viral disease characterized by the appearance of skin eruptions |
| **Sun Dance** | the most important of Kiowa religious rituals, held yearly and lasting for three days |
| **tai-me** | the most sacred of all Kiowa spiritual objects |

# INDEX

## ABOUT THE AUTHOR

TERRANCE DOLAN is a writer and editor living in Brooklyn, New York.

## PICTURE CREDITS

Courtesy of Maurice Boyd, *Kiowa Voices: Ceremonial Dance, Music, and Song, Vol. I* and *Kiowa Voices: Myths, Legends, and Folktales, Vol. II.,* Texas Christian University Press, 1981 and 1983: pp. 46, 49, 52, 60, 64; Courtesy of Carson County Square House Museum, R. C. Cline Collection: pp. 34 (bottom), 38 (lower left and lower right), 39; Courtesy of R. C. Cline Land Co., Inc., R. C. Cline, President: p. 38 (top); Courtesy of James and Helen McCorpin: pp. 40 (top), 62; Missouri Historical Society: p. 34 (top); Courtesy of N. Scott Momaday: p. 73; Museum of the American Indian/Heye Foundation: p. 33; National Anthropological Archives, Smithsonian Institution: pp. 10, 12–13, 35–37, 42, 58, 70; National Museum of American Art, Smithsonian Institution, Washington, D.C./Art Resource, NY: pp. 16–17, 44; U.S. Department of the Interior, Indian Arts and Crafts Board, Southern Plains Museum and Crafts Center: pp. 3, 6, 19, 22, 25, 30, 40 (bottom).

Maps (pp. 28, 54, 66–67) by Gary Tong.